THESE WILD HOUSES | Omar Sakr

THESE WILD HOUSES
OMAR SAKR

CorditeBooks

First printed in 2017
by Cordite Publishing Inc.

PO Box 393
Carlton South 3053
Victoria, Australia
cordite.org.au | corditebooks.org.au

National Library of Australia
Cataloguing-in-Publication:

  Sakr, Omar
  These Wild Houses
  978-0-9752492-7-7 paperback
  I. Title.
  A821.3

Poetry set in Electra 10 / 14
Cover design by Alissa Dinallo
Text design by Kent MacCarter
Cover illustration by Lily Mae Martin
Printed and bound by McPherson's Printing, Maryborough, Vic.

10 9 8 7 6 5

To Judy, for your guiding light;
to the friends I made family.

I couldn't have done it without you.

Contents

What will survive of us? Not houses. If left alone, they begin to fall apart very quickly.

–James Woods

Preface

As-salāmu ʿalaikum.

I won't keep you long. First, I acknowledge the Gadigal people of the Eora Nation, on whose land the majority of this collection was written.

Now you are about to read the poetry of an Arab Australian, which is a rare thing when it shouldn't be. Now you are about to read the work of a queer Arab Australian, which is a rare thing when it shouldn't be. Now you are about to read the life of a queer Muslim Arab Australian from Western Sydney, from a broke and broken family – not rare, but it should be.

This is not a definitive statement on Islam. This is not a definitive statement on Arab identity, not Arab Australian identity, not bisexuality, not even Western Sydney. It is a statement – an exploration of me and what I've seen.

The only thing I ask of you is that you do not stop with me. Discover the other diverse writers and poets in this country – find us, find our books. We're here, and we're growing.

–Omar Sakr

Introduction

Omar Sakr's *These Wild Houses* is a complex exploration of identity, an identity exposed in clear yet layered language, a language that takes us to the core of what he has experienced as a 'queer Muslim Arab Australian from Western Sydney, from a broke and broken family.' Given the rarity of Australian poetry written from these particular perspectives, and given that all these labels still carry stigma and disadvantage, you might think that you could guess the tone and content of the poems from these biographical details. You might expect anger, rage, resentment, bitterness, poems that rail against prejudice and injustice, and while these emotions do feature in the work, they are tempered with compassion, warmth, tenderness, understanding and supple perceptions. In the first poem, 'Door Open', Sakr welcomes us in to his world: 'Come inside, let me / warm you with all I am'. And he does warm us with his intimacy of voice, his inclusivity, his emotional diction.

There are many references to houses in the volume, and for Sakr these are important sites: places in which we can come to terms with who we are, places where we learn the stories about ourselves, and among other things, where we can experience displacement, cruelty, neglect. In 'ghosting the ghetto' he tells us how in 'their third floor brick flat, the one tucked into the asphalt folds of Warwick Farm … my grandparents were rebuilding Lebanon'. This beautiful poem with its long-breathed lines and confluence of rhythms explores generational change and the way in which Muslim and Australian worlds collide and intersect: 'Beirut became Bondi became Liverpool, & the local creek behind the cricket pitch / drank the old rivers, and new names blessed our flesh: Nike, Adidas, Reebok.' In many poems he delves into complexities and complications that arise from coming from a multi-cultural background. In 'All My Names', he says 'I never knew / what to do with all my names, these silhouettes, of a boy I never was or wanted.' Throughout the book, houses and rooms are metaphors for states of being; as he says in the final poem, 'A house should, above all, be still.'

What strikes me especially in these poems is the way in which Sakr grounds his work so indelibly in the body. He knows thoroughly that the body is the primary house, the one in which our identities are irrevocably caught: in the skin, under the skin, in the heart.

In many instances this knowledge is rhapsodically transformed, as in these lines from 'What the Landlord Owns':

> ... unfamiliar language
> is no barrier when you dwell on the borders
> of domesticity, when the soft hands of the sun
> sculpt the sloping muscles of a man like sand
> as he mows the lawn, and hair muzzles
> his face

Sakr's poetry consists of rich and convincing detail charged with presence and particularity; his poetic voice is so firmly planted and immersed in the world around him that the urgency of his images and rhythms is completely convincing. Sakr never summarises or straitjackets the emotions; instead he allows the tonal range of his voice to surface through layers of astutely organised rhythms and imagery.

These Wild Houses is an impressive debut, a collection which announces a new and important voice in Australian poetry.

–Judith Beveridge

AHLAN

Door Open

Like all habitats, my body tells.

Wild houses we
live in licked brick & sun
warmed stones, in grass blood mortar
& flesh. Listen up the halls, be careful
with floors; carpeted with pine,
tiled joy wanting. Come inside, let me
warm you with all I am. Mind your head
here on the ridges of my teeth. Careful
where you step, I am breakable – never
mind the wallpaper claiming otherwise.
Onto my polished tongue,
there flies and fiction breed
into some thing resembling a truth.
Here, at first, my history begins.

Here Is the Poem You Demand

Here is contested ground, the soiled
earth at my feet.

Here is uncouth domestic abuse & plasma televisions,
the marbled fruit of my skin.

Here is the assumed socioeconomic background,
its backyard barbecues, its books, the blues.

Here is the un-italicised flavour of my tongue: jahash!
This is a song we have sung before and will sing again.

Here is the heat you desire, the tender cock,
the hardness at her core. The taste and twitch of it.

Here is the mosque you despise, minarets pinked
by sky. Never forget it in the foreground

no matter its size. These things are all about perspective.
Here is the forever tree bearing the bodies of loss.

Here is my name, over & over & over & over.
Repeat it until you get it right, until it calls.

Here is the noose I hang myself with
every day. Here is the blade I trust will sever it.

Landing

My grandparents flew here homes ago,
their wingspan besting oceans to reach
where worlds end, and begin again. My
mother and her siblings, while fledglings

only, retained their feathered bodies
a movable Mediterranean. They spoke
as prophets, mellifluous and mysterious,
warping westward as the children grew

into forgetting, close enough to clip
their echoes, but far enough to mistake. Our first
hopped steps and outstretched arm beats
lamed the same breeze that once gusted

theirs to elsewhere. Shadows tallied behind
my grandparents' eyes when they watched us try and lift.
They'd say, 'You do not know what it means to take,
to rip your roots from clay and craft them into sails

ready for the sky.' I would have answered
if waves hadn't taken my words. They remain
darkened by their old sun, carrying country distant
cedars on their backs. In their rush, I wonder

how much was left to blubber in sand, and if they took
to air as skeletons of bleached bone, leaving history
behind for the gulls to pick at. Grandfather, no craters
cradle my feet, there is no war here, only family,
yet I cannot find a purchase on your landing.

Dear **Mama**

Don't preach to me, Mama, don't tell me no stories
about some holy book-er-other, about angels, devils and
jinn. I've learned too well already the religion of your fists
and my body's drummed its song, its bruised gospel
so often it knows no other, and at night I garble
the chorus, gasps interspersed with bass and moans lowed.

Your god is capricious, strikes no reason, some days (the hours
you had full gear, I later found) you'd grin and order us a pizza
in and we'd lounge about our smoky temple as your silver screen
apostles entertained us, shot & bled & fucked & spat & died
for us. Those days were best. Others were nails-on-chalkboard,
a kind of possession at the edge of hearing – your cheekbones, jaw,
elbow, everything was knives and cut against the air
even though your teeth were set, lips locked prison-tight.

A tinnitus, only I could hear it, but I swear your body screeched
those mornings loose with warning, and so we learned to read
your augurs in Dunhill smoke, those exhales prophesying pain
if we didn't become paragons of silence. Sometimes even then.
You saw my treacherous father in the closet of my skin, my face
his imprinted sin.

I remember when the locksmith came, his confusion, dawning
pity when he asked, 'You want the lock *outside* his door?' Your cash
and a small gold chain sealed my cage. How could you think walls
would hold me? If only you knew how I made that cell a world, hard
but free, you might refashion yours: a hundred books, each one key.

I ought to thank you, dearest Mama, for the prayers
I memorised, the blessing of hunger, and the urge for independence
you sang into my bones, percussion-deep, the taboo calls of meat,
the need to roam. I ought to thank you, dear Mama, for your piousness,
for showing me the cruelty and beauty of a God and godlessness
all combined, and for teaching me that holiness is no more
than moments lent with loved ones whether bonded
by blood or not. Especially not. I ought to thank you, Immi, but I'm out now
and the mosque is empty.

After

The morning after the burial, we
ushered in dawn with unleaded,
driving along ice-rimmed roads
to the cemetery. The newly dead
need comfort, like five-year-olds
on the first day of school, Mum
said. The sky was discoloured fruit
fingered out of misted windows
into which I breathed & shaped
a name.
      We stumbled out
the car onto cracking grass,
then arrowed in upon the grave,
a small uneven rumble of earth
& rock blued by winter's halves.
I might as well have been alone
as I stood above Teyta's home.
I saw the rumpled soil parting
for me, a dirt sea for grief
and its stricken Moses

                    descending
into the spacious kingdom of after.
Below, I would hold her chilled
hand, soothe her worries, and still
her fearful shaking. I would
wait with her in the dark
for the angels to arrive, bearing
a visage of light or else
black eyes & hammers spiked
with judgement.
                    I would be fearless
beneath the beat of thousandfold wings
as they hurl their holy questions.
I would allow no harm to befall her
regardless how she answered: I know
too well there are no devils here
who do not work for God, only angels
wearing masks to suit the moment.
I imagine this so often in the years
that follow, I forget
                    who are the winged
there to question, who is being held
as gently as a newborn, who owns
the grave I rest in & the name
on its tombstone.

The H Word

My suburbs had hoods, baggy low-riders, we
all did. Around our necks, they hung

loose in the heat, rode high in the rain.
The alleys became the Hume then, a kind

of tunnelled vision: that this is all there is,
pockmarked streets and swollen knuckles

for homes, another H word.
The scariest one. Not horror or homicide

or haemorrhage or hate. Not hope.
Home.

If your home is haemorrhaging kids
into open graves and closed cell blocks in a flood,

pull your hood up. Hide your face.
Your feet will still be wet with red

correctional pens. It's hard to field
humour when hunger eats away your family,

when all you have is stale bread. 'Put sauce on it,'
my cousin said. It goes down

easier. Hood the suburbs, they go down
easier. It shouldn't have surprised me, but when homo

was added to the spread, everything hurt
just a little more. I came to map Hell,

every inch beneath my skin. Still, when days cool,
a hoody is my go-to. Sometimes

it keeps me warm. I pull tight the cords
to strangle sounds in my throat.

But even if I cannot speak my lips still frame it,
awake or asleep, crooked as hips

bent on hooking for a little H
on the side. The word is *help*. The day I die

I expect to look down and discover in my chest
a hooded heart, lying heavy and still.

Not So Wild

In the mornings I'd loiter outside your house,
shivering in the thin mist, breathing out
your name & waiting for you to fill it.
You'd blink and stutter in the new light,
stretch and yawn as morning gold washed
over the loam of your skin. 'What now?'
you'd say and we'd begin, two small boys
absent reason but full of need
a wordless urgency that ran the length of our sleep.
I never answered, would shrug and let the day
respond as we marched down a rock-strewn road
that muttered with each step, scatting to the beat
of every tyre treading over it.
                                    Drawn down
to the lodestone creek – brown, barely burbling,
but full of tadpoles and tiny frogs to snatch at,
we echoed the soft throb of their croaking.
Losing ourselves in the steep trenches, we
left them each time a little less tame, naturalised,
shaggy with weeds, brambles, the occasional thorn
and cobweb. Some days you came out of the house
crackling with storming boyhood, furious
without cause, cursing every leaf and branch
and stone – why are we here, why do this now?
Small wonder, I never knew what to say, cupped
wriggling worms in a small pool of mud
to distract you instead,
                                    to lead away
from your abrasions, the screaming matches
everyone heard but chose to swallow, knowing
our own houses were tinderboxes and the roar
of their flaming would come sure as the sun.

Some weeks I'd be the one requiring silence
and the wonder of some thing in the mud
or stuck beneath the weight of a boulder
or carried off by a belt of industrious bull ants.
All we had was each other, a mirrored heat
simmering in summer. Do you remember
any of this?
                            Do you recall
the way we grew into each other? The days
we followed older boys to the water tower,
a bloated toad of ruddy metal on the hill,
and watched them summit the top, tatters
of porn clutched in hand? You scrabbled
after them once, and I could only watch,
cemented to the ground as you ascended.
That was always your specialty: every day
you built anew the wings burned and beaten
off your back, an Icarus, but always
able to rise again. My own body remains
flightless. Sometimes
                            I dream-sing
you adrift into riotous clouds, and feel
again the joy of those formless days.
Only now am I unloading this quiver
of questions, a feathered wilderness.
You returned from the sky changed
somehow, older & wiser & immeasurably
distant – whole worlds spun between
our almost-touching fingertips
as we walked home. Every morning,
the road connecting our houses has been empty
of us, its music reserved for other boys.

THE LIVING AND SINGING ROOMS

Botany Bay

On a grassy plain overlooking Botany Bay
two men pray, facing the East
kneeling to sea. Children windmill
around the spit of land, squinting
in the heat as seagulls, bellies puffed
and ready to fight for scraps, tear
at each slim gift.

Blankets anchor double dates
on the green, the pebbled cliffs and sand.
Fish and chips steam in sun.
A couple walks with bánh mì
in hand. Before me is spread pide, eggs,
cucumber and focaccia. Over there, my aunty
says, is Captain Cook's museum.

Through the haze, it looks both close
and awful in its distance, a thin bridge
connecting it to us. My grandmother,
too worn by salt and earth and time
for the rigours of prayer, just sits
rocking, faith on her split lips and skin.

Imagining the invasion, I lie upon blades
of grass, staring up at the hijabbed sky
footprinted with clouds and wonder
what Cook would have made of all this.

this girl, this country

Overheard in the local supermarket:
'you can take the girl out of country, but you can't take the country outta her'

not the mountains or the rivers or the coal,
never dirt or loam. the girl is
its history, she is the lynching and the rape,
the stolen generation, the thief, police,
the mother and the father. the girl
cannot remove the cliff face from her skin,
the shoreline from her spine or coral reefs
cutting her spleen, no matter how dedicated
or how much she bleeds. the girl is brume,
is bracken, the girl is beast & bushfire's
body.
                     her landscape is untimed,
a cycle of ravage and renewal, a country
which curves the ends of earth
in a pair of denim jeans, the girl encompasses
even the clouds. the girl is wind, not here
nor there, but stuck somewhere in between
trying to slip the physical, her occupied flesh.
when one girl meets another they come together
as two parcels of land, and if they look
into one another, they'll see a national park
peeking out one eye, or an indigenous council
meeting in a stolen house. the girl is other,
is the ground beneath us, is the air
our lungs pump, invisible, indivisible
and necessary.

the girl was poetry, often forgotten
her formation and features trodden, voice subsumed
in the hubbub, the burble of creeks, language
segregated black and blue country
flags stitched up night, veils to hide the casualties
of warring. the girl was loved we said
so in song & oath & vow, loved so strong
we killed for her, whether she willed it or not,
we killed.
                    folkloric, the girl remained
the crushing wheel of law, the advancement of australia
fair. she haunted our textbooks, headlines, homes
our buses, servos, offices. we knew the girl
was dying because she told us with her first & last
& only breath; countries strung in miniature, in flesh, blood
and bone, they died all the time, and we did nothing,
thought the land would always be. over & over we were
told, as statistics grew over her gassy corpse,
that her immortality was at its end, that girl,
this country, and still they said, it's just her time
of month, a seasonal ruin, that's the way things are.

Election Day

Savour the day, there is no more important a message
than that. Suck its marrow out, swirl it along
your tongue, the sweetness in calm, stillness. Even
the dawn is slowed, it seems. This is the day the spin stops.
These few hours are all you're allotted to find your feet,
to ditch your swaying sea legs, the blue-tied back of politics.
This morning, get the bitter jab of Arabica beans
knobbing your mouth, nose, throat. Anticipate the heat
to come. Water the flowers before you forget
and everything is reset to blur, dying coral reefs
and hirsute miners in fluoro vests digging up some femurs,
refugees mired in valuable rock. Men kissing men,
ministers palming crooked money (& also kissing
men) and hysteria everywhere, hijabs and halal kangaroos,
child abuse covered up here, here and here, recurring
beneath so many creeds you can layer
a horrible rainbow
                      Just water the damn flowers
is what I'm saying, and walk down to your local
town hall or public school, lose you in the eruption of language,
a bright-winged battle of parakeets and magpies, crash-hot
and do your best to slip past the pitched tents of war;
anything immovable in this uncertainty is not to be
trusted. Go past the sunny child holding up his parents'
placard – his naïve bliss an incandescence,
unaware his future isn't girt by sea, but consumed
by it – and there, in the hushing echo, rustled newsprint
and muted coughs, cast your voice into spin. Fate
will have with it what it wills. As individual faces
merge into almost familiarity & engines gun
through street music, brace for hurtling
the motion of upturned Casula, to hear your future
announced in monotone drones on touch screens –
brace hard for the impact of changing everything
and nothing.

All My Names

Forget the empty hearth – trail your hand
along the mantle, watch these portraits:
my gap-toothed smile, gangly arms,
lingering cheeks. For my rainbow teeth
they called me Changeables – for the skull
towering over my unfilled frame, Pumpkin
Head. One of my uncles adorned my crown
with the title *effendi*. He said it meant friend
in Turkish, not nephew. I never knew
what to do with all my names, these silhouettes
of a boy I never was or wanted.

> See my cousins too, Jalal, walnut brown
> & already balding somehow, his sister
> Curly Sue. See Fatty, see Jemz, see
> my brother, my aunt, my family
> out on the housing-commission streets.
> This is important, too, what kind of house
> you live in: shambling, McMansion, flat
> or tool shed? It matters to children
> and adults. Though rented
> for a time, these houses leave scars.

ghosting the ghetto   for Steven

In their third floor brick flat, the one tucked into the asphalt folds of Warwick Farm, past El Toro Motel, down where the winding road straightens out opposite takeaway tucker, my grandparents were rebuilding Lebanon, and no one seemed to mind. Every Sunday we made like pilgrims in Holden Commodores, traversing highway homeland

to bicker and eat. As adults renewed rivalries, we kids splashed in the Abraham River, once known as Adonis, an ancient baptismal turquoise that cleaved through the hallway. Sometimes the country changed with us & we climbed Mount Lebanon in the lounge, cooling our bodies beneath old olive trees.

The tapestries were gaudy, the TV a small cube in the corner, and smoke was forever on the air. In that, metaphor & country are one. As with every hajj, there were too many bodies and the door was kept open for us to spill from, an ecstasy of difference. In this, metaphor & Arab are one: no lone place can hold in its small clay hands so many rivers

and no ark can contain us, whatever scripture commands.

In adolescence, the Kaaba flowered between us, a black square lotus edged in gilt across the sides, doors of gold gleaming in afternoon light. It made ants of us the mountains and rivers, the motels and the convenience stores. Now we spoke by rote prayers half-memorised in the sacred hours of the insomniac, sinking budding secrets

and the kinds of questions that can unmake family.

When the girls started to stand apart, trying to hijab their modesty, we saw *jamarāt* all around us, & lined our hands with bits of rock to hurl at the devil. Only the walls were a mirage and it was our cheeks that split beneath thrown stones. Later, it made perfect sense to learn that in 1627, a gutter was added to the *Kaaba*

to protect it from flooding. Or perhaps to stop it from blooming.

Before my grandparents began to recreate Lebanon out of ruined cartilage, someone should have checked if they were students of history, or if they knew their way around a map. Beirut became Bondi became Liverpool, & the local creek behind the cricket pitch drank the old rivers, and new names blessed our flesh: Nike, Adidas and Reebok.

Someone should have checked if they knew a flower could replace the house of God.

Boys have no business with God, except where he can be found in the slap of hard feet on concrete, in the seismic collision of shoulders and hips lunging for the try line, or the throng & buzz of bees and wasps among long grass and thin weeds; or sticky lips locked on lips in the secret space beneath houses. Boys have no business with God

until their bodies lengthen and sin begins to stick to their tongues.

Soon after, our weekly hajj halted. Our family became families and rupture became familiar.
In this, metaphor & Middle East are one. In the long months away from that imagined country,
I heard of an older cousin, a name hushed by others, a man in love with men, and in his absence
I saw my future: who knew you could ghost the living?

Who knew you could bury the ghetto in forgetting?

I am unearthing yesterday, ungathering this bouquet of quiet, reappearing
in inches. Lebanon was left incomplete in Warwick Farm, & everywhere else we went
the ragged tops of mountains peeking out of windows; the Sacred House in fragments,
in bloodied bits of stone, in black and gold petals on the floor. Though the builders are gone,

they left the blueprints in my skin, every alley & every river, every ghost & every ghetto.

All In

The barman at the club delivers drinks
with a smile, asks if I'll write a poem
on the napkin I require. If I'll stain
this small white space. I can't
think of a reply, and in the pause
that follows, we grow uneasy
at the idea that what transpires
here might outlast the moment.

Wiping sweat off swarth,
I walk back to the bank of TVs
by the poker table in the corner.
In front of small screens, old men sit
in mute wonder, glued to the moves
of athletes in their prime,
the explosive lunges of sweat
slicked youth wrestling on
grass, hungry for glory.

It takes time, the unwinding,
but gradually they become younger
skin slimy and new in reflections
of limelight as fresh rage
jacks their rapture. *Ref! Pay attention!*
I'm caught up in ageing rapids, a Benjamin
Button in reverse, aching for quiet to return,
to enjoy my drink, the forgetting it brings.

Behind me, a scuffle erupts. *Say it
in English, I dare ya*, spits a grizzled man
over the rippling dialect of chips
and a smattering of Arabic. After,
an official oozes over the speaker:

> *Remember, only the English
> language
> is allowed at the table.*

It makes sense, really.
At a poker table the cards
you hold are irrelevant. All that matters
is your bluff & theirs, what you are
willing to accept. I keep drinking,
staring at the screen as two other
Arabs move away from this white space
without having stained a thing.

Call Off Duty

Salaam, brother. I am rekindling
when last we met: your body knotted
into a fist around the controls, screen aglow.
'Search & destroy,' came the instruction
and your fingers fired, the machine gun
your only avatar on screen. It speaks
in bursts of you, and men fall prostrate
as if praying, echoes of the azan
bowing on the air.
                    The fading sound
called for submission, but though I've seen
your head hit the mat in the unfolding
choreography of prayer, the blaze within
you never dimmed even for a moment,
not then, not now, as duty urged
you to kill with such ease then laugh
at your victory, glee and vitriol flowing
from your lips.
                    Samson, our dog
gambolled wildly at our feet, fur unshorn
and gossamer thin, fey-lit with ghost light.
Sweat gleamed on your brow, and you growled.
Occasionally, face set, hackles raised.
Only when your phone pulsed and sang
God's song did you press pause, then turn
to see if I'd wash with you.
                    I demurred,

and you laughed. 'Still on the fence? No?
What are you then?' I didn't answer, brother,
busy submitting to struggling, to overcoming
reality. Salaam, I accept you'd prefer
the fantasy of death and fury given form
than to speak to me; I too barely know
the comfort of family, or how to sow the fields
between us with things green and grateful.
Salaam, I know when you discover my secret
loves, I will lose yours, and the ache of knowing
it gnaws at my bones, this loss I have
yet to bear.
                    Salaam is knowing
your hatred is foretold, inscribed in Arabic,
in the holiest of text; it is knowing the morning
will dawn when you pretend not to know
my name, when you won't look at my way.
Salaam is loving you anyway. I'd rather
fold myself into a supernova's flare
than submit to this, it's that hard to think
of a life long without your laugh. But
the day is accumulating, driven closer
with every poem I write like this & I write
every day, even now, snug in the corner
as you play on cold, serene in the chaos
of your virtual world.
                    Brother, salaam

I must ask: if I cover my body in verse
you cleave to, will you see me then? Maybe
later, when you honeysuck the East, your mouth
gracing the Earth, you will know me in full
or at least make the effort to try. Some would
say that if ours is peace – accepting paths
twinned from the start are set to part – I should
make war and gut your wisdom,
the weave of your life. I'm not sure
if you would survive the breaking
of all that you think you know. This is me,
brother, mine, saying I forgive you
for all that is to come, and hoping
at last for salaam to exist between us –
in this life, or the next
                    as the light tapers
out, I hit 'send' on this letter of years
in the making. You reply: 'Don't be
silly. I'll always have your back.'
And everything I thought I knew
broke into a sound like prayer.

THE IN-BETWEEN PALACE

Wallpaper

Note the paintings on the walls,
moments pig-stuck in time,
a collage of firsts – some hazy
with motion, a blurred thumbprint
obscuring the view, some sharp
as starlight – a fumbled kiss, lips thick
as rubber gloves, the first skull I bruised
my knuckles, the disgust in a boy
as he called me dirty
Lebo, said to go back
to wherever I'd come from
(and don't think he meant the heart
of exploding stars).

Detour

Inspired by 'Since I Left You, Baby' by BB King and Katie Webster

The blues been spinning a long damn time,
& I have heard this talking jazz intro
so often I mouth it, a lip sync to wilting:
a duet, in this instance. Katie sings
life is hard & she's tired, tied, sped.
I'm walking up the road as her waves
wash against me, the air itself soggy,
the night fat and full with our heft.
Lights flash in the distance, shouting in
morse code tongue, but the blips fuzz
as though drunk. I let the meaning
sort itself. Focus on getting there
first. BB's guitar complains in the dark,
her voice sharpens like a lover's,
liable to cut your throat: *Now,*
I'm intelligent enough to recognise
a detour sign, but I'm hard-headed,
she says, and I see roadworks ahead,
giant arrows directing cars to some other
slant of moonless track. I laugh, stunned
by this meeting of song and life and road
in soot-stained skin, in idle wandering.
I wasn't in a car though, the cues were
irrelevant, the circumstance burgled
of significance. I just kept going, past

the trucks blocking the way. Ahead,
the road was bathed in harsh light
like a body staining a gurney in a morgue,
only the medics here wore fluoro vests & tatts
danced up their arms. Chunks of highway
were stripped bare, revealing the tender earth
that wants beneath all our great works,
that waits to cover them again.
Machinery hummed and women swore
and Webster sang her woe
as I watched industry at work. Further up,
the road gleamed with a slick new finish,
its blackness wet and gloating. Two men
hunched and talked, hard hats screwed on,
a third lay outstretched on the sidewalk,
asleep or dead, I don't know. They paid him
no mind, neither did I, and I stepped over
his emptiness, over the earth scattered
everywhere, getting into my fucking
shoes, foreshadowing the future.
I don't have an end to this jive no
resonant arc or thematic consummation,
like me, it just had to get out
the way BB must play and Katie sing;
I'm telling you because it happened.
And coz the blues demand payment.

America, You Sexy Fuck

You're wearing your prettiest dress:
Fall, the only one named
for its desired effect, that is
when the colourful fabric (succinct
golds, russet and deep browns
swirling together) slips
to your knees. The trees
are endless skeletal shadows
blurring the horizon,
some clinging to a final vibrancy,
daring winter to preserve them
still crowned in aspen glory.
The view out the window shifts,
gradual as the seasons, the inclines
of forest recede, and clusters of homes
wink out from the foliage – humanity
emerging from living acreage – as of old. Roads
proliferate, black stretchmarks
stitching your limbs together.
Factories punctuate the distance, the smoke
hanging between chimney and sky, still
as a painting, yet drifting apart slowly
like a cloud. Destiny beauty-marks
your collarbone (the dress pools
as you reveal yourself to me) sign-posted
at an intersection near Syracuse; I had the rare
pleasure of watching Carver diminish
in the rear-view mirror, not a destination,
merely one of many ways making
inroads into you. Fat syrupy

clouds gather, swallowing the blue
and you begin to sweat red.
I cross your bridges, your rivers
and gorges patterned with cottonwoods,
tracing my footsteps across soft Dakotas,
sweet-talking a groove into your crops.
I want to peel them back with my teeth,
see what's beneath, what you're hiding,
but I'm too distracted by your brazenness,
the swell and heat of your hips. A valley
between and a vast wetness appears: steam
billows off the lake, perhaps it's fog *this* dense
rolling whiteness unbuttoning the cuffs
and trailing fingers over lips of storm.
I am heading to your politics,
walking New York, singing Michigan,
whetting my tongue on your discrete edges.
Tell me, can I outline your everything?
Between us, lies, so much emptiness:
pit stops, Detroit Burger Kings, and dead towns
spoil the tree line
with a beautiful kind of desolation.
Beautiful because of people like Tammy,
iron-grey and swinging sixty, still working
behind a counter, smile manufactured in '89
who keeps industry alive
well past its use-by date,
the way winter rips off autumn heads
highlighting its beginning
in a furious burst of colour.

THE LAUNDRY

A Communal Wash

New laundries, like houses, remind us
to erase, to begin again skin-fresh,
to reflect no matter the method, be it
launderette, in-house box, riverbed,
two-storey townhouse, duplex, shanty.
Bring your filth, your shame
expunged for 150 cents, no more,
though it goes up every year,
harder every year, our sins calcified
into teeth, an internal inflation system
we carry with us, distributing sediment
and old pains. In this way, bodies
contain echoes of their old form,
distant aches, twinges, remembered
fucks. Hates. If only we could
stuff countries up in here, soiled
cities and resorts, and iron out
the ugliness stitching flags together.

Comin' Out the Station

Coke cocks the freeway, leering red
familiar as a screw and easy as
to forget: the magnitude of it, the intensity
before it fades. Anyway, it's the legs –
naked outlines lit in pink this place is
known for, bada bing these Xs lined
in rows, never mind the Os. The smell
of pide too, the heaviness of baked bread,
the dank reek of beer, a crossroads
with an aftertaste
                         strong as a fucked mouth
in a toilet stall by a twiggy twenty
-something whiteboy in skinny jeans,
the neon burn slicking his skin
in a blue sheen. The ache of being
on your knees lasts forever – just
ask any priest. Braced at the intersection,
I am surrounded by unwanted signs,
undesired people, a colony
of seagulls whirling above
                              as the ground
grits its unpicked teeth, shreds of knotted gum,
twisted buds poking out like weeds beneath
my feet. Down the road, I know Samoan Peter
waits to cut my hair, his soft hands at ease
in their strength – he shapes my features,
shepherding the shifting pieces of selfhood
into reunification
                       or at least the semblance
of one. That will come, I know, a kind of flooding
to parch this arid stretch. The seagulls sense it too,
it's what they've been waiting for all this time;
the colony disbands into fragmented white dashes
as the light yields to a permissive colour
and I enter the Cross at last.

On the Cnr of Holden St, Ashfield

As he kneels in the shadow of the steeple,
his rough-sketched hair meeting brick,
the man's features are blank stone bags
surrounding his body like traffic cones
his irrepressible life spilling out in bright
unwashed clothes. The wooden doors
of the church are shut, green paint flaking.
Faint singing thrums inside as cars recite
past, metal and glass afire beneath the sun.

The occasional silhouette deepens
the shade gracing his crown. Black birds
flip from a nearby telephone pole, barking
holy verses at pedestrians who duck and glide,
a ballet of avoidance, this dance of never
looking up. The man does not look
up, nor does he hear the winged hymns,
steeped as he is in the bliss of stopping
for a while, comforted by a man-
shaped structure that doesn't shy from him.

The stone wall cradles his cooling,
he leans into it, flesh and brow
praising mortar at the hip and shoulder,
his form of prayer.

Echoes of Home

The *snikt* of metal catching and refusing to flame
The ashen tumble of Mum's words around a fag in her lips
The dog's lingo invading the yard with the fallen tree
The car coughing its way into the driveway
The TV muttering in its dotage, colours hotter than cartoons
    Grandfather sitting in front of it, lungs rumbling with soot
My brother machine-gun spraying the walls with laughs
The rustle of pages chasing one another to the edge of morning
The slapping of hands on spit-slicked cocks in the night
The moon's restless cycle laying hands on bare shoulders
The wind slashing its name on skin, its history on collarbones
The joyless chittering of bats in the trees, raining ripe pits onto stone
The street inhaling and exhaling Indian mynas, some other birds
The collision of exuberant kids in too-narrow hallways, crowing victory
The concussion of bass turned up to mask the applause of splayed thighs
The chuckling of lawnmowers long resigned to repetition
The pings of landlines crying out for release
The rasp of tissues muffled by the secret folds of midnight
The beating of fan blades smacking against the heat
The sizzle of zinc roofs, the whiskeyed singing of corrugated iron
The scraping of chairs around the dining room table
The *azan* heaving God's words at dawn, the possessive notes of prayer
The swish of hooded women gliding past, their tongues a sweetened hook
The muted thunder of a cousin's snores tangled in his beard
The caterwaul of voices circling in the kitchen
The whispered sleepover, a tumult beneath blankets gone off
    Mangled English in the air, then my throat, thick with Arabia
The sombre cadence of news anchors, ceaselessly AM and PM
The mailboxes fingered by postmen
The fritz of the television switching off, the bang of the remote falling
The coming and going of all that I miss
    resounds in my Inner West apartment.

A Visitation

Like a traveller in my own body
stay only for a while, heedless
of the cost to the original owner.
Break it down, piss on the floor, fling
sonnets at the moon like scat, make love
wherever feasible – spend yourself simian,
open up for others to empty into you
lost in the ecstasy of yes.

Some day I will pass through
here from now into later
this place will be empty
for a time, until the original owner
claims it back, and blades of grass
peek out through the slats.

THE WIDE OPEN

Trees Don't Pay No Rent

Plant yourself deep, Mama, I heard
Centrelink is coming for you.

The warrant has been issued
& the sheriff is putting on boots – quick,

get in this hole I muddied with my mouth,
chewing out space for your tobacco-stained roots.

Never mind the worms, put your feet in
this wetness. Centrelink is coming.

Think tree-thoughts, Ma, drink the sun.
Aunty always said you'd a green tongue.

I can hear it already, your hair's a bird's nest,
all snarled in verbs, a tangle of bitter syntax.

The sheriff is nearing, eviction papers in hand.
Fresh-made kibbeh nayeh idles on the table

and morning light glints on munted mince
when he arrives, but you're nowhere

now. Just me sheltering in a tree,
its body supple yet tough-skinned,

a mother's camouflage.

A Familiar Song

'Ladies and gentlemen, if I could have your attention, please —'
His strong voice commutes throughout the carriage.
Coming out its station, at first it could be anyone speaking,
even God itself. *'My name is _____ and I am homeless.'*
I cannot find this homeless Allah past the crush of bodies
but I've heard this song before, over surging music
& a jazz scat heartbeat. The refrain is always on
even if verses change:

'Listen, I used to own a pretzel cart. Life was good
until I was hit by a car last year and the hospital took everything
in exchange for my health. Now I can barely stand.
I walk with this cane and struggle to work.
If it was just me, I wouldn't care, but I have a little girl
a little four-year-old girl I can't bear to see me beg.
I am a proud man. I was a proud man.
I hate to beg but please, anything you could spare,
please, would go a long way.' Here comes the slow
shuffle, the shake of the cup, the click of cane,
the deafening vacuum of sound the rest of us are.

'Listen, my name is _____ . A rare bone disease is eating a hole
into my right side. My wife is working two jobs trying
to support me and we still can't afford the surgery
I need. I worked hard for 35 years & it wasn't enough.
I'm sorry, so sorry to be disturbing your day,
but I'm out of options. I hate to beg. I am a proud man.
I was a proud man.' The chorus boots in, interrupted
by opening doors, the squelch of disembodied voice:
'This stop is 34th St. Next stop is 42nd and Bryant.'

Then comes the corpse walk, the mien of the broken;
IV tube snaking in and out of his pack, it disappears
into his shirt. Listen: limping Iraq is next,
then the bearded Kabul, their voices gash
shrapnel, but now everyone's stares glaze
and it's harder to hear them. Vietnam
has stopped trying to persuade the subway:
he only lingers on its platforms for warmth,
until staff herd him out into another cold. None of these
remnants speak to each other; they compete
for the same ration of hard audience.

There's this immigrant woman too, she does not speak,
merely holds up a sign with one hand, a despondent babe slung
in the other, head lolling. She sifts silently among us,
a disapproving spectre, a widow perhaps, a mother
of quiet tugs at the imagination, invites speculation.
She does not trust herself to speak, to unlock
her mouth, lest it release its long scream coiled inside.
My friend gives her coins, says, *Okay, that one's hard
to ignore*, before returning to an unsinterested state
as another nameless singer gets by, kicking in a chorus
again, and I realise my hands are clenched claws,
the scream held back is mine because I am
a cash-strapped scribbler and I have nothing to give
except. What I am. Listen, my name is _____ .

Harmony of Dirt

Grief's first touch goosed my tender skin when a car
took my dog by chance. I thought I knew death then,

but still stumbled over its name. We got closer
when my cousin Samir was killed on the streets

of Liverpool. Dizzied by the tangible absence
of a body I used to know gone to grass,

I thought it was here at last, but we were only casual
acquaintances at best. No more, less. Before

I turned 24, my cousin Jamal was born premature.
I met him in the morgue attached to Lakemba

mosque. I recall thinking how convenient that arrangement
was, how economic the slip between life and death,

the footpath between worship and loss
made manifest. The tiny baby boy was not blue

but instead a pale white, as of snow.

All around him a circle of bearded men stood confronted
with finality, a father with son,

a cousin with cousin, life with echoes.
His funeral made a Friday morning

and the sun shone while a small hole was scooped
back into the grave of his grandfather. They said

this way the old man's spirit would protect him
or else the boy's innocence would cleanse sins

off his ancestor, I forget which. Maybe it was both
and past & future met in the dirt. The next morning

my grandmother, diagnosed to die months
ago, finally passed. As if she'd been waiting

for her great-grandson to illuminate the way, or else rushed
onward to take his palm and lead him to after.

I no longer had to wonder about death, my old friend
passed out cold in the room it spent my lifetime building,

a DIY home reno in my chest
full of familiar faces. I nursed it

as a mother would, coming to understand
and love the new contours of my body.

How could I not when it took the shape of family?
In the lull of conversations, I hear their voices open

a song of wounds. When I stop
to listen in full, I'll know again the kindred tune my body

taps into rhythm all across the world's wanting
& life will build in harmony of the dead.

What the Landlord Owns

I should tell you about my other house,
the bricks, I mean, the building not the metaphor
gunned to its breaking point. It sits atop one
of many hills in Ashfield, squatting on the edge
of an intersection, the large structure split into
three duplexes. Three families. The three
now live where just the one once
waxed wood with childhood memory. I sleep
in the master bedroom, window facing out
towards descending rows of backyard. At night
their square lounge-room lights are strung out
like cheap smack, like baubles on a string
for the cat to bat. I know the stringent cry
of the neighbour's wife and his mumbled pleas
as well as I know my own waistline, despite
their different gauge; unfamiliar language
is no barrier when you dwell on the borders
of domesticity, when the soft hands of the sun
sculpt the sloping muscles of a man like sand
as he mows the lawn, and hair muzzles
his face, but you know the cut of his jawline well
enough to shave him in the dark. I sit at my desk
breathing deep the pungent spices of their dinner,
the cold scent of their arguments while shadows
clothe the hallway of my home and I see
that hunger precipitates movement. Steep
stairs make descent dangerous, I take them at a run
when I can no longer stand empty. The dining
table is covered in books, old and new,
the words of dead and women gathering
dust, their resurrection in me a matter of wait.
The oven can only be lit with a tapering flame
coupled with a prayer, the fridge so old it sing-speaks
Langston and the go-go washing machine
has the laughter of a tap dancer trapped

inside it flits with every task it is set. Two minutes on
is all it takes to heat up a meal before I return
to my window, desk and the strait of stars
guiding surf in the dark above these families
living near, unaware the house and light on the hill
are ruptured within, choking with three separate ways
of silence.

A Biographer's Note

A house should, above all, be still.
It becomes problematic when home folds,
as Baba Yaga discovered – no one is easy
with the idea that at any moment, you could
become their neighbour, if only
you chose to stand.

Why even our homeless
could be afforded the same dignity as you or I,
what is tragedy and how might it play
to see a life where now we recoil
from the stink of desperation?

Notes

'ghosting the ghetto'

The *Kaaba* is a building at the centre of Islam's most holy mosque, Al-Masjid al-Haram, in Mecca. It has many names, including Sacred House, House of Allah and House of God in Heaven. All Muslims pray towards it, and to which they must undertake the hajj, the journey to it, at least once in their lifetime.

As part of the hajj, Muslims perform a ritual known as the Stoning of the Devil, in which they throw stones at three pillars known as *al-jamarāt*.

Acknowledgements

Some of these poems were published or made possible by the following: *Cordite Poetry Review, Mascara Literary Review, Meanjin, Overland, Tincture Journal,* Red Room Company, Right Now Inc. and the ACU Poetry Prize.

Thanks to Judy Beveridge, for her patience and generosity, and the workshop group who continue to tolerate my first drafts. To Peter Minter and Toby Fitch, for awarding 'Not So Wild' runner-up place in the Judith Wright Poetry Prize, and to the Malcolm Robertson Foundation for funding that generous award. To Sam Twyford-Moore and the Emerging Writers Festival, for being so supportive and fostering life-long connections I will always treasure – I am in great debt.

Special thanks as well to Najwan Darwish for taking an interest in a fledgling poet across the world, and for taking the extraordinary step of having my work translated into Arabic and published in *Al-Araby Al-Jadeed.* The gift of another language is impossible to measure, and I am humbled by it.

Omar Sakr is a bisexual Arab Australian poet born and raised in Western Sydney. His poetry has been published in numerous journals, and his non-fiction has appeared in *Archer, Going Down Swinging, The Guardian, Kill Your Darlings* and *The Saturday Paper*, among others. He placed runner-up in the Judith Wright Poetry Prize (2015), and was shortlisted for the Story Wine Prize (2014) and the ACU Poetry Prize (2015).